T
Hill That Grew

Esther K. Meeks

ILLUSTRATED BY LAZLO ROTH

ERNEST BENN LIMITED · LONDON

Dick got a sledge for Christmas.
"Good!" said Dick.
"I like sledges."

There was snow on the ground.

Dick went out to play
with his sledge.

Ann went out to play too.

Ann was Dick's little sister.

Dick pulled the sledge.

He gave Ann a ride.

He gave Ann's teddy bear a ride.

He gave Ann's doll a ride.

But no one gave Dick a ride.

Teddy bear could not give Dick a ride.

The doll could not give Dick a ride.

Ann could not give Dick a ride.

Ann was too little.

Dick met Tom.

"Look!" said Tom.

"See what I got for Christmas. My sledge is just like yours."

Dick said, "Good! We can play together.

Sledges are fun."

Dick gave Tom a ride.

It was a good ride.

Then Tom gave Dick a ride.

"Sledges are fun," Dick said.

"But it would be more fun if we could both ride."

Mother came out.

"Mother," Dick said, "Tom has a new sledge just like mine.

We like our sledges.

I gave Ann a ride.

I gave Tom a ride.

And Tom gave me a ride.

But we can't ride together."

Mother said, "I'll help.
I'll give you a ride together."

Dick and Tom got on the sledge.

Mother pulled the sledge.

"That was a good ride,"
said Dick.

"It was fun," said Tom.

Mother said, "I must go in now. I must get dinner ready."

Tom gave Dick another ride.

Dick gave Tom another ride.

They gave Ann and the teddy bear and the doll another ride.

They all made a snow man.
Then Father came home.
Father laughed at the snow man.
Father found an old hat for
the snow man.

Dick said,

"Daddy, Tom has a sledge just like mine.

Sledges are fun.

But how can Tom and I ride together?"

"I'll give both of you a ride," said Father.

He gave Tom and Dick a good fast ride.

He gave Tom and Dick and Ann and the teddy bear and the doll a ride all together.

"This is fun, Daddy," Dick said. "But how can we ride together when you are not here?"

"I know something that would help," said Father.

"But it's something we don't have in our town."

Father thought and thought.
He talked to Mother.

How could they help the boys have fun with their sledges?

Father talked to Tom's father. Everyone thought and thought about what they could do to help.

Dick's father and Tom's father went to see Mr. Mayor.

They said,

"Mr.Mayor, our boys need a place to ride their sledges.

Can you help?"

Mr. Mayor thought and thought.
Then he went to see Mr. Builder.
Mr. Builder built houses.
Big houses. Little houses.
All kinds of houses.

The workmen had to dig away the earth to make room for the basements.

The earth was piled up around the houses.

Mr. Mayor said,

"The boys in our town need a place to ride their sledges, Mr. Builder.

I have an idea. Will you help?"

"I'll be glad to help,"
said Mr. Builder.

Mr. Builder told the men to put the earth on trucks.

He told them to take the earth to the park.

He told them to put all the earth in one place in the park.

As the men brought more earth, a hill began to grow.

First it was a little hill.

Then the men brought more and more earth.

The hill grew and grew.

Before long it was a big hill.

When it snowed again, snow covered the hill.

One morning, Dick's father said, "Come with me, Dick and Tom. Bring your sledges. We are going to the park."

Tom and Dick had a big surprise when they got to the park.

"Look!" said Dick. "A big hill!"

"A big long hill!" said Tom.

Boys and girls were going down the hill on their sledges.

Mr. Mayor was there with his two boys.

Mr. Builder was there too.

Everyone was happy about the hill.

Dick got on his sledge.

He gave it a push.

Tom gave his sledge a push.

Down the hill they went together.

"Hills are lots of fun," said Tom and Dick as they climbed up again.

First published in Great Britain 1962
Second impression 1965
Third impression 1970
Ernest Benn Limited
Bouverie House, Fleet Street, London, EC4

Printed in Great Britain
by Jarrold & Sons Limited
Norwich

ISBN-0-510-09206-3